HOW TO ELIMINATE DEPRESSION
AND
NEGATIVE THINKING

BY:

GABRIEL NEWMAN, Ph.D.

gtn

A Product of:

gtn

GTN Publications
P.O.Box 65203
Baltimore, MD 21209

ISBN: 978-0-6151-4354-5

www.gtnpublications..com

Dedication:

Chaya Tamar

First,

One and only.

The Light of my path.

With thanksgiving to the Creator

Table of Contents

Chapter 1

Can You Overcome Depression and Negative Thinking?

You bought this book, reaching out for help, indicating that you really want to overcome, or get rid of, this thing in your life. You surely must want this a great deal. You seem to believe, or at least will entertain the possibility, that you can overcome the monster.

I have good news, better news, and then some bad news for you. Which should I tell you first? Okay, here's the good news:

The Good News

This is not a hocus-pocus book. It is the real thing. You did not waste your money.

- Most of what you will read in here is based on solid data – the latest in research from the world of psychological studies and clinical practice. The author is a trained and experienced psychotherapist, with a PhD in Psychology and many hours of clinical work, working for years to help people like you. The content of this book is a synthesis of both clinical experience and that which is known from valid, scientific studies – of the latest in research findings.

- My experience also includes spiritual leadership to congregations, in which I've worked with thousands of people suffering loss, loneliness, guilt, grief, or pain. I have counseled many of these individuals, taught mental health professionals in the area of grief, and listened to personal stories of pain and depression, as well as stories of triumph over depression. This, too, provides a basis from which you can benefit.

- And, like the Men's Hairclub guy used to say: I am not only the president – I am also a customer. I have used the system outlined in this book to eliminate depression from my own life, as well as the lives of many with whom I have worked. So I know it can work.

The Better News

You can do this by yourself. You will not need hours and hours on a couch, in a psychotherapist's office. You will not need to spend hundreds of dollars on equipment, drugs, memberships, or trips to hotels and conferences. You CAN try this at home; …in fact, I beg you to try this at home.

The Bad News

The bad news is this:

I cannot do it for you.

Nor can your mother, husband/wife, manicurist, or hairstylist.

There is only one person on earth who can get rid of your depression: YOU. And it will require some work on your part.

Now, if you are **<u>not</u>** willing to do the work, then indeed you wasted your money.

But, if you are willing to work at it, you can make this the opportunity that changes your life, and transform your inner, mental space to a happy, positive place. After all, that's where you live, and where you spend all your time. Might as well fix the place up a bit.

So, let's start by getting a better understanding of our enemy - this greedy monster called 'depression'.

In the back of the book you will find pages dedicated for your own note-taking, to record points, or your own thoughts as you go.

The mechanism - All Roads Lead to Gloom

The mechanism of depression is actually easy to understand. It just needs to be explained well. Stick with me through this, and it'll become clear to you. Here's a common experience that most of us have had; if you can identify with this, you can understand the neurological and chemical process of depression.

A man leaves his house to go to work every morning, five days a week. Leaving his driveway, he makes the same left turn, followed by a right turn. He stops at the same intersection, waits at the same lights...all this, without thinking about it. In fact, he's not even aware that he's not thinking about it! His mind reverts to an auto-pilot mode, instructing his body to respond to the cues around him, while he thinks about other things. He travels the same roads every day, responding to cues, or signals, with the same movements each time. Whenever he sees that convenience store, he automatically puts on his turn signal, then makes the turn immediately after passing a gas station. Meanwhile, he can be planning his next date, or working his mind through a thorny problem at work. Next, he automatically starts making a turn into his parking garage right after a red brick building, barely even thinking about it. Now, imagine that one particular morning he does not have to be in the office, so he leaves the house to meet a friend at a coffeehouse. Before he knows it, he finds himself halfway to his office, realizes his mistake and turns around to go back, cursing his stupidity. But he is not stupid. He is simply human, doing what most of us have done, not once, but many times over. This incident has probably happened to you, in one form or another.

Well, that same process of auto-pilot functioning is going on all the time, in our minds. We are always traveling mental pathways that are automated, pre-programmed, set by years and years of repeat travel. We don't realize that we're in this mode, when it's happening, but it is going on.

So, let's simply substitute the destination – the man's office - with a state of mind (depression), and the roads leading to it with well-trodden mental pathways that bring us to that same end point, over and over again. Is it conceivable that a person might simply steer herself to the same place, time and time again, without even realizing she is doing it? If the end point is depression, there are many possible 'triggers', or pathways leading to this destination. It could be an external, provoking factor – as when someone speaks to us in a nasty way, depressing conditions in our house or office set us off, or dismissive parents put us down at every opportunity.

These are like the originating signals or cues that start us out on the path to an end destination. When very well entrenched, it's not only a path that's well-trodden and well greased, it's more like a steep hill downwards. Once we start that downward rush, it's almost impossible *not* to speed to the bottom, 'crash and burn'.

So, if the mental pathways leading to depression are well traveled, we develop both *external* and *internal* cues (these concepts will be explained fully in Chapter 4), that direct the automatic twists and turns in our thinking, until we simply land up right back in that depressive state, without even realizing that we're on our way. While on the journey, we're generally not aware that alternate pathways even exist – if we're in auto-pilot mode, how could we ever see forks in the road, or alternate pathways? We convince ourselves that anyone else, in our circumstances, would respond with the same feelings. This appears to us, in the situation, as a self-evident truth. An unshakeable reality.

But it's not.

Just as the man on his way to work could choose at any time to alter the route, to travel in a totally different way, to stop for coffee, or park halfway there and walk the rest of the way, we can likewise choose to alter the mental pathways along which we travel. The first requisite: we must know that such choices exist! That there are alternatives.

Even in the simple realm of our metaphor - the daily commute - we often lose sight of our choices: we forget that we could take another route to get there. We could be exploring our neighborhood, try new pathways, and perhaps find a much more scenic route. In fact, with regard to the daily commute to work as well, this is often advocated, to avoid boredom, and to keep our minds stimulated. So, all the more, we need to explore alternate pathways of the mind, to experience more freedom and personal control.

Will it be easy?

No. Trying new routes, you're bound to get lost, to drive up blind alleys, or waste many precious moments trying to get out of circles that lead nowhere. You'll have the discomfort of being in unfamiliar territory. BUT...and it's a BIG but...you could also discover a whole new way to live. Different ways of doing things, different frames of mind to live in, different people with whom to interact. You might encounter interesting new places that you never knew existed. And, ultimately, the unfamiliar can grow as comfortable to you as the familiar once was.

You have to be willing to explore new ways of doing things, and be less predictable, to yourself as well as others!!

First, you have to believe that the familiar, the comfortable little depressions, the mental negativity and sadness which you've carried inside you for years, perhaps even your whole life, are not the best pathways for you, in the first place. **THEY'RE NOT YOUR FRIENDS.**

Depression, negativity – this is a horrid place to be, for it tends to paralyze people, and fill them with fear, and a constant sense of foreboding. By purchasing this book, you demonstrated awareness of the fact that you acknowledge this – that you'd like to effect change in your life. Can it happen? Is it possible to change this 'reality'? That depends on one thing, and one thing only…

Did you hear the light bulb joke regarding psychotherapists? It goes like this:

Question: How many psychotherapists does it take to change a light bulb?

Answer: Only one, but the light bulb has to really, *really* want to change.

The punch line applies here, too. If you want the change, really want it, you can make it happen. But only if you want it enough. You can reduce the levels and frequencies of depression, then reduce them further. With time, and determination, you could even eliminate this unproductive, debilitating state of mind from your life completely.

Will it be easy? No, it will not be easy. You have to take control of a thinking process that is invisible to you. You have to wrestle with your own internal mental process, and with automatic ways that you've used for responding to life and its situations, for years.

*But you **can** do it.*

This book will show you how to identify the steps, and how to implement them. You simply have to want it enough, and follow through. And after that, start living with a brand new, positive outlook on life that will help you realize all the dreams and expectations of your heart.

At this point, it's important that you gain a picture of your own internal state, by answering a few crucial questions. A quiz, let's say, to establish your current baseline in depression. Please take a few moments to answer the questions below. No-one need see the answers but you. Answer these questions as relative to the past week. During the past week:

1.	I was bothered by things that usually don't bother me.

0 – rarely or none of the time

1 – Some or a little of the time (1-2 days)

2 – Occasionally or a moderate amount of the time (3-4 days)

3 – Most or all of the time (5-7 days)

2.	I did not feel like eating; my appetite was poor.

0 – rarely or none of the time

1 – Some or a little of the time (1-2 days)

2 – Occasionally or a moderate amount of the time (3-4 days)

3 – Most or all of the time (5-7 days)

3.	I felt that I could not shake off the blues even with help from my family and friends.

0 – rarely or none of the time

1 – Some or a little of the time (1-2 days)

2 – Occasionally or a moderate amount of the time (3-4 days)

3 – Most or all of the time (5-7 days)

4.	I felt that I was not as good as other people.

0 – rarely or none of the time

1 – Some or a little of the time (1-2 days)

2 – Occasionally or a moderate amount of the time (3-4 days)

3 – Most or all of the time (5-7 days)

5.	I had trouble keeping my mind on what I was doing.

0 – rarely or none of the time
1 – Some or a little of the time (1-2 days)
2 – Occasionally or a moderate amount of the time (3-4 days)
3 – Most or all of the time (5-7 days)

6.	I felt depressed.

0 – rarely or none of the time
1 – Some or a little of the time (1-2 days)
2 – Occasionally or a moderate amount of the time (3-4 days)
3 – Most or all of the time (5-7 days)

7.	I felt that everything I did was an effort.

0 – rarely or none of the time
1 – Some or a little of the time (1-2 days)
2 – Occasionally or a moderate amount of the time (3-4 days)
3 – Most or all of the time (5-7 days)

8.	I felt hopeless about the future.

0 – rarely or none of the time
1 – Some or a little of the time (1-2 days)
2 – Occasionally or a moderate amount of the time (3-4 days)
3 – Most or all of the time (5-7 days)

9.	I thought my life had been a failure.

0 – rarely or none of the time
1 – Some or a little of the time (1-2 days)
2 – Occasionally or a moderate amount of the time (3-4 days)
3 – Most or all of the time (5-7 days)

10.	I felt fearful.
0 – rarely or none of the time	
1 – Some or a little of the time (1-2 days)	
2 – Occasionally or a moderate amount of the time (3-4 days)	
3 – Most or all of the time (5-7 days)	

11.	My sleep was restless.
0 – rarely or none of the time	
1 – Some or a little of the time (1-2 days)	
2 – Occasionally or a moderate amount of the time (3-4 days)	
3 – Most or all of the time (5-7 days)	

12.	I was unhappy.
0 – rarely or none of the time	
1 – Some or a little of the time (1-2 days)	
2 – Occasionally or a moderate amount of the time (3-4 days)	
3 – Most or all of the time (5-7 days)	

13.	I talked less than usual.
0 – rarely or none of the time	
1 – Some or a little of the time (1-2 days)	
2 – Occasionally or a moderate amount of the time (3-4 days)	
3 – Most or all of the time (5-7 days)	

14.	I felt lonely.
0 – rarely or none of the time	
1 – Some or a little of the time (1-2 days)	
2 – Occasionally or a moderate amount of the time (3-4 days)	

3 – Most or all of the time (5-7 days)

15.	People were unfriendly.

0 – rarely or none of the time
1 – Some or a little of the time (1-2 days)
2 – Occasionally or a moderate amount of the time (3-4 days)
3 – Most or all of the time (5-7 days)

16.	I did not enjoy life.

0 – rarely or none of the time
1 – Some or a little of the time (1-2 days)
2 – Occasionally or a moderate amount of the time (3-4 days)
3 – Most or all of the time (5-7 days)

17.	I had crying spells

0 – rarely or none of the time
1 – Some or a little of the time (1-2 days)
2 – Occasionally or a moderate amount of the time (3-4 days)
3 – Most or all of the time (5-7 days)

18.	I felt sad.

0 – rarely or none of the time
1 – Some or a little of the time (1-2 days)
2 – Occasionally or a moderate amount of the time (3-4 days)
3 – Most or all of the time (5-7 days)

19.	I felt that people disliked me.

0 – rarely or none of the time
1 – Some or a little of the time (1-2 days)

2 – Occasionally or a moderate amount of the time (3-4 days)
3 – Most or all of the time (5-7 days)

20.	I could not "get going".

0 – rarely or none of the time
1 – Some or a little of the time (1-2 days)
2 – Occasionally or a moderate amount of the time (3-4 days)
3 – Most or all of the time (5-7 days)

….Continue reading only after having completed the quiz…

The above is a widely used test, created by Lenore Radloff at NIH, and referred to as the CES-D (stands for Center for Epidemiological Studies – Depression).

Scoring this test is easy: simply add up your answers. If you were not sure on any of them, take your higher score on that item.

A score of 9 or less indicates someone not in depression, and below the national average; 10 to 15 would be mildly depressed; 16 to 24 moderately depressed, and over 24 indicates heavy depression – at least, during the past week. But, please bear in mind: this is only a general guide, not a way of diagnosing yourself. **Only a mental health professional can make a true diagnosis,** based on history and many other factors. Your purpose in taking this quiz is to know how many symptoms of depression you might be expressing CURRENTLY, and to establish a baseline.

If you scored in the upper range (16 and up), you clearly want to start implementing this book in your life as soon as possible. Devote much energy and effort to doing so, and do not let anything deter you from it. This is your life!

If your score is between 9 and 15, great news, you're not in a full-flung, critical, four-alarm depression right now. But, it's there, and probably holding you back, as it fluctuates up or down. This program can definitely free you, and grant you much higher productivity.

For those who scored under 9, assuming you're not living in the land of denial, this program has the capacity to bring you a whole new level of power through positivity.

In all cases, please retain your total score, above: you will find it interesting to refer back to it later in life.

Now it is time to get to work on changing things. Ready? I hope so. We'll try to have some fun along the way – please don't take offense at any humor. Of course, if you **want** to take offense, I can't stop you; it's a free country!

Chapter 2

Recognizing the Symptoms of Depression.

Having answered the quiz in the former chapter, you already have some familiarity with the symptoms, and what we might look for to determine if a person is truly suffering from clinical depression or not. All the same, a chapter devoted to the topic is well justified, so that you can begin to know what the signs and symptoms are, to recognize them in yourself or anyone else, for that matter.

So, here's the official description of depression, as codified in the all mighty DSM –IV (DSM stands for Diagnostic Statistic Manual, otherwise known as "Bible of Psychiatrists". The IV represents the fact that it is the fourth version, or revision, of that manual):

Five of the following nine symptoms would justify a diagnosis of Depression, provided there is no physiological cause (for example: some medications cause lousy mood, so do thyroid conditions, anemia, and a host of other physiological conditions):

1. Depressed mood.
2. Loss of interest in usual activities.
3. Loss of appetite.
4. Insomnia.

5. Psychomotor retardation (which means slowing of thought and movement)

6. Loss of energy.

7. Feelings of worthlessness and guilt.

8. Diminished ability to think and poor concentration.

9. Suicidal thought or action.

So, quite simply, if you answer "yes" to five of the items listed above, and there is no other reason for this low mood, you might be suffering from depression.

One aspect of the above list that should probably be adjusted, is number 3 – loss of appetite. After all, we all know that some lose their appetite when depressed, while others tend to eat more. So, instead, it makes better sense to say: "significant change of appetite". Likewise for sleep – depression can cause either lack of, or excess sleep. However, as you simply look over the list above (which is definitely not carved in stone), realize this: low affect ('lousy mood') is what depression is about, and it expresses itself in behavioral changes. Naturally. Who ever felt great about themselves when they were feeling down? Who ever had a great get-up-and-go attitude when they were low? Logic, and common sense, should rule. And, you probably know which of your behaviors is likely to change first when you're feeling low. Do you retreat, like a recluse, and eat ice cream until you throw up? Do you sleep all day? Sit frozen in front of the TV? My point here, quite simply, is that you don't need a guru, or 'expert' with a crystal ball to tell you that you are legitimately, officially, medically, specifically, clinically, definitely, depressed. You know.

What I like about the CES-D quiz, given to you in the last chapter, is the fact that it focuses on your inner world – your emotions, and your perspective, instead of a list of "symptoms" that psychiatrists voted to be the exclusive signs of this condition. The CES-D was designed to measure <u>current</u> depressive symptoms, and especially depressive affect. The 20 items were carefully chosen, a sort of 'best of' 5 earlier depression scales, to represent all of the major components of depression. These include: depressed mood, feelings of guilt and worthlessness, feelings of helplessness and hopelessness, loss of appetite, sleep disturbance, and psychomotor retardation (slowing). Many are familiar with the Beck Depression Inventory; it is better administered by a practitioner, rather than self, and its focus is more on symptomatology towards diagnosis, rather than internal feeling.

Just bear in mind one other aspect of the definition in that famous (notorious?) DSM, which is important. It calls for the condition and feelings to have been present for at least two weeks in a row. Imagine someone being sad for a period of ten days, and we rush him into hospital, declare him suffering from clinical depression and give him drugs and therapy. He may be a little sad, but we'd be certifiably insane! Obviously, the condition has to have been around for a while, and not looking to go away in a hurry.

Demographic Description.

Who gets depressed? Depression has been referred to as the 'common cold' of mental health because it is found in high number in all segments of the population. Twice as many females suffer from depression as males: the prevalence of depression has a range of 9% to 26% for females, but only 5% to 12% for males. Is there a genetic component? Well, maybe. Major depression seems to be 1.5 to 3 times more common among first-degree biologic relatives of people who suffer from depression than among the general population, according to the Diagnostic and Statistical Manual of Mental Disorders (American Psychiatric Association, 1987). But this is not a very impressive number, in the world of statistics, and it does not represent cause. We are often misled by such findings: it is possible for another factor common to these relatives to be causing depression in both of them. In other words, do not overlook the power of 'state of mind' in bringing about these depressive feelings.

The special vulnerability of teens.

It is estimated that about 20% of teenagers are suffering from, or will suffer from depression in the course of their high school period. Well, that's not much different than the rest of the population, you may say. True, but the problem is the manner in which teens respond. Suicide is the third leading cause of death among teens, and our guess at this point is that depression is behind the vast majority of these deaths. This, because teens do not have the inclination to "talk it through" as much as adults, and tend to believe that life will not improve; they are also aware of ways in which they can act on their suicidal impulses. Thus, any signs of depression in teens must be related to with great seriousness, and should never be ignored. No matter how much teens protest that they want to 'be left alone', the adults around them cannot afford to do that. GTN Publications will be offering a special manual regarding the application of this program in teens later within the 2007 calendar year.

Chapter 3

Anatomy of a Depression.

Understanding the neural and chemical process of depression/negativity, the action of anti-depressant drugs.

In the interest of understanding the mechanisms behind depression, we're going to get a little technical in the next two chapters. Don't let it scare you too much. It's not absolutely crucial to successful implementation of the program in this book, and you will not need a PhD to do this. In fact, if you truly wish, you can skip the next three chapters and go right on to the program, in Chapters 6 and 7, coming back to read this section at your leisure. However, a slightly better understanding of how depression and negativity work will definitely help. The better we understand our enemies, the more competent we get at beating them! You can, of course, choose to come back and read these chapters several times over later, even as you begin implementation of the steps towards your taking control of the big-toothed monster known as depression.

The first major switch I want you to make is in your view of the phenomenon we call depression. From now on, think of depression as: a **response**. Response, but not a reflex, or reaction.

Start thinking of a negative or depressive state as an option…
therefore a behavioral choice…**one** of the available alternatives in
a given situation. It's a path we <u>choose</u> to take. Like a verbal response (making a certain statement), or a physical response
(dancing the jig, or hitting someone), it's <u>one</u> available response out
of the pool of infinite ones available.

Whoa! Please, don't shout at me! I hear many of you answering back:

"What do you mean it's a choice? You think I *like* being
depressed?"

Or: "What of the chemistry? Have you totally forgotten
about the fact that there's a bio-chemical process? My doctor told
me it's because I lack certain neurotransmitters that I'm depressed."

Or: "This has been in my family for centuries. Millennia.
Since my ancestors were cavemen, squatting somewhere in the
Adirondacks, sucking on bones, they've been depressed, so don't
you go telling me…"

We'll get to all these issues. But first, let's take this slowly, one step
at a time.

Let's explain this concept a little better, in all its components:

A: The Road More Traveled – Neural patterning

Neurons that have been fired frequently are in a state of readiness to fire again. This is one of the reasons for our difficulty in breaking out of a certain pattern of thought. You know how your mind tends to work a problem, or situation, over and over? Not because it's devising new solutions to deal with it, either, but simply because you're not managing to stop yourself. We get to the point where we're sort of locked in to a behavioral repertoire.

Or, here's another example of the same phenomenon: remember how you start using a certain word, then find that same word inserting itself into your speech, even when you try not to use it? Or: notice how when your hand makes a certain mistake in writing, like leaving out a specific letter, it will keep doing that within the day, and you cannot figure out why it insists on doing that? All these occurrences stem from neural patterning – the neural pathway most recently fired becomes the one most likely to fire again. The road most recently traveled becomes the road your mind wants to travel.

Is this bad news? I guess, if you're thinking that it restricts our freedom of choice, and compels us to do the same thing over again, regardless whether the action is good or bad for us. It's also a good thing, in the sense that we could not live without it. Remember our man on his way to work in the morning? It would be as if he was learning how to get there, every morning afresh, if it never automated itself into his behavior. Habit, mental patterning, is what allows us to become really skilled at something, when we do it over and over again. Ask Tiger Woods, he'll tell you.

So, we've hit upon a great secret.

A magic potion.

A really important clue to your unlimited power.

YOU CAN REWRITE BEHAVIORAL CONDITIONING, SO THAT IT WORKS <u>FOR</u> YOU, NOT AGAINST YOU.

If our behavior is limited to, and strongly influenced by, paths taken in the past, does this not mean that we can influence it now, as well, by creating, then reinforcing, new pathways? This has to be a two-way street, no? Just as paths selected before can dictate from the past, so can they be dictated to, and then dictate differently into the future, based on what we choose now! All we need do is select a different pathway, and then travel it, many times over, to release ourselves from the grip of the past. Just as repetition can work against us, it can also work for us, provided we decide to be the boss, and take it in hand.

YOU CAN REWRITE BEHAVIORAL CONDITIONING, SO THAT IT WORKS <u>FOR</u> YOU, NOT AGAINST YOU.

There's no fatalism in this, as long as we still believe that we can operate with free choice. To rephrase a famous saying: *<u>we have nothing limiting us but the belief in limitation itself</u>*.

B: The 'Grease' on the Road, or: Chemistry of Depression 101 – The Cooperative Oompa Loompas

Our society is really into quick fixes. Why invest effort, and many hours, when you can fix a problem in one second, with the right pill? So, when drugs like Prozac, Zoloft, Paxil, and others came along, a big, country-wide party began. What a neat solution! We could manipulate our moods, elevate our sense of wellbeing, even enhance our productivity and efficacy at work, by popping a little pill once or twice a day!

Let's evaluate just one of the theories behind chemical manipulations of mood. About thirty years ago, we identified a neurotransmitter called **serotonin** ('neurotransmitter' simply means a chemical that helps carry electrical messages from one neuron to another in the brain, like bridges across rivers). We figured out that serotonin is somehow related to depression. Like dopamine, and norepinephrine, two similar such critters, it seems to influence mood. We assumed that if you have less of it than you should, you get depressed. Along came the SSRI's (**S**elective **S**ynaptic **R**euptake **I**nhibitors), which delay the clearing out of serotonin from synapses (meeting points of neurons – the bridge spot).

Basically, we all have a clean-out crew inside us, that comes along to sweep the neurotransmitters away from the synapse after they've done their job. The SSRI's cut off the cleaning crew – the reuptake agents - at the pass; they prevent the clean-up crew from doing its job.

Examples of SSRI's are: **fluoxetine (brand name: Prozac), fluvoxamine (Luvox), paroxetine (Paxil), and sertraline (Zoloft).**

Two SSRI's that work on both serotonin and norepinephrine are: **venlafaxine (Effexor) and nefazodone (Serzone).**

Simply put, using SSRI's extended the action time of serotonin. So, it's kind of like increasing serotonin in the system, without actually increasing it. Well, we were all tickled pink when the SSRI's seemed to help people suffering from depression, and our chests were puffed out in self-pride. Can't argue with success, right?

And just as there are reuptake inhibitors for serotonin, thus are there as well for dopamine and norepinephrine, the other 'happy' neurotransmitters.

Example of a really effective Norepinephrine and Dopamine reuptake inhibitor (NDRI): **Wellbutrin**.

Then there are the tricyclics. No one really knows how or why they work; we speculate that maybe they, too, block reuptake of the 'happy' transmitters. But then, that's the problem with most of the neurotropic drugs (drugs that work on the brain): their benefits were generally discovered accidentally, which means that we don't know how or why they do what they do, but the simple fact that they seem to help will cause doctors to prescribe them a dime a dozen. The tricyclics are also beneficial, it appears, for ADHD and several other conditions.

Examples of Tricyclics:
- **Adapin or Sinequan (doxepin)**
- **Anafranil (clomipramine)**
- **Elavil or Endep (amitriptyline)**
- **Ludiomil (maprotiline)**
- **Norpramin (desipramine)**
- **Pamelor (nortryptyline)**
- **Pertofrane (desipramine)**
- **Surmontil (trimipramine)**
- **Tofranil (imipramine)**
- **Vivactil (protriptyline)**

Well, there are side effects to all these drugs – not as bad as they used to be, when the drugs first came out, but not insignificant, either. These can include: dizziness, vision problems, bladder problems, constipation/diarrhea, nausea, dryness of the mouth, and much more. You either suffer from the side effects, or you don't.

On the other hand, a doctor who has about five to ten minutes, in a good scenario, to try to help someone get relief from an insidious depressive state – well, why wouldn't he/she prescribe, if it could help you? It would be irresponsible **not** to do anything.

But, what if our original assumptions were wrong? What if the process is more complicated than we thought? You see, the neurotransmitters are not tiny engines driving our systems, deciding which mood we should be in. I mean, look at them! They're nothing but little messenger-boys, delivering the impulse from one neuron to the next!

It is more appropriate to see the neurotransmitters as basic equipment of our system, ready to serve whatever mood the system chooses. It ain't the boss, it's the servant!

It is far more appropriate to see serotonin in a dynamic role, responding to changes on a constant basis, and as one of the tools being influenced by mood. It might be helpful to think of the chemicals and neurotransmitters in our brains as cooperative little critters, like Willy Wonka's Oompa Loompas, doing whatever our system needs them to do.

For an analogy, think about adrenaline. We need that rush of adrenaline for the high action moments of our lives; thus, when we exercise, run for the train, or find ourselves in a risky, challenging situation at work, there is dramatic increase in the adrenaline released into our systems. It actually feels good (once you get over huffing and puffing). But, too much of that, on an ongoing basis can lead to heart attack or heart disease, and will certainly fatigue and age us prematurely. All of us enjoy the sensation of increased adrenaline – it provides a sense of mastery, excitement, and strength. That's why many people engage in risky behaviors, simply for the sake of the adrenaline rush that comes with it. Others bring about the same sensation by taking drugs (caffeine being a mild example of this) that simulate the good feelings of high adrenaline.

Did you know that there's a safe, legal, perfectly healthy way to create the same sensation? In fact, it's actually very good for you. It's called: exercising. A good, old fashioned bike ride or jog, does wonders to alter our inner chemical make-up, and it is doing so honestly, in the sense that it provides energy to a system that really, truly needs it. Our bodies were smartly designed to give us the strength and energy that we need, when we need it. More about that in Chapter 6. Any artificial means of creating that same sensation is,… well, artificial. It is unnatural, and there's almost always a price to pay for these artificial manipulations of our bodies.

Likewise, when it comes to our friend serotonin (or dopamine, or norepinephrine): we have thought of deficiency in these 'happy' neurotransmitter critters as an abnormal, chemical condition that *causes* depression. So, pop a pill. Add a little serotonin to your system (or prolong it in the system), and you'll feel happy.

Too simplistic. In actual fact, the chemistry drives the mood and is driven by the mood which drives the chemistry which drives the mood, which drives the…you get the picture, I hope. Take a look at the diagram below; hopefully this will clarify somewhat the interactive, cyclical nature of our moods, our behaviors, and our inner chemistry and psychological triggering.

The more complicated dynamics of how this operates in our bodies is schematically represented in the table below; it is important to understand that a change or interruption in any one of the four quadrants will cause change in all the other three – thus, it is possible to influence things by changing the environment, or by changing how one responds to the environment, or by affecting the inner chemical process, or by changing one's behaviors in the given conditions that prevail. Consider the structure depicted below:

$\longrightarrow$ Environmental stresses and forces	Inner feeling of depression, low mood $\downarrow$
$\uparrow$ Depressive behaviors, leading to…	Chemical make-up for depressive state $\longleftarrow$

Logically, it makes sense that we should be able to interrupt this process at almost any point in the cycle, to bring about change. Chemical intervention is one way; behavioral change is another; shifting the 'inner world' is yet a third way. So, the contention of this program is that whether or not you are using drugs to uplift your mood, you need to work on the other two (inner world and behaviors), at least in tandem, if not 'instead of'.

Bear in mind that we have no idea, really, how we might be affecting the system in harmful ways, long term, when we take a neurotransmitter, or some form of facilitation of a neurotransmitter. After all, our system is made with loop-backs, in which it gives itself feedback all the time. Thus, if we take serotonin orally, the system will say to itself "Oh, there's plenty of that stuff floating around, I can shut down production for a while." Thus, all factors point to the notion that this is not a wonderful long-term solution.

Bipolar Disorder: Different from the rest.

It is very important to distinguish between the other forms of depression and bipolar. Bipolar involves two phases: a manic phase and a depressive one. In the manic phase, the person flies high like a kite. They are convinced they can do anything, handle everything, and succeed at whatever they try. During this phase, they will often start many projects, buy equipment and sign up for courses, or start new business. However, along comes the depressive phase, and they 'crash'. No energy, totally depressed, they feel like they cannot do anything. As a result, they often suffer great monetary loss, and lose friends and marriages. After all, who can live on such a roller-coaster forever? Those who believed in them during their manic phase (they are very convincing at those times) will invariably be disappointed, even feel betrayed.

Bipolar conditions are believed to be biological in origin, and therefore **need** to be treated with drugs. Thank God for lithium, a wonderful stabilizer, that brings these folks back from their extremes, to ground them in the center. They dare never stop the drug use, and can certainly combine that with a program like ours, if they so choose, to avoid depressive patterns of thinking during that part of the cycling. It has serious warnings, especially for potentially expecting mothers, thus it has its limits.

Not everyone responds to lithium well; for others, it has been found that an anti-convulsant may help them. It goes by the name of Carbamazepine, or the generic Tegretol.

What of the rest? Well, the unipolar depressions will certainly have a portion of genetic contribution involved (where it carries down in the family through genetic transmission)– but these are the minority. By far the majority of depressed people in our society suffer from "psychological depression", which is what this book seeks to address and eliminate. Consider this your handy merry-maid service, here to sweep away those depressive feelings!

Chapter 4

Drugs: To Do or Not To Do, That is the Question.

Considerations regarding use of anti-depressant drugs arriving at a strategy that works for YOU.

This leads us to asking a really important question, that simply must be asked: should we be absolutely opposed to drug treatment for depression?

Not necessarily, and certainly not initially. For some, this is a short cut towards a much more bearable existence, and a real chance to turn their lives and emotional tone into something more positive. For someone suffering from very severe depression, all the other recourses (therapy, positive psychology, change of life-style…what-e-ver) simply may not be powerful enough to start the turn-around, not unless the chemistry is first reset, to give them a fighting chance. One of my favorite expressions that has relevance here: *sometimes life is just bigger than therapy*. This doesn't mean we give up. No, Siree. It just means we start with a little boost, an extra, temporary hand up, in the form of these drugs, that really can work well. The mistake, in my opinion, would be to rely on them as the only, and complete solution, which they are not.

Also, we sometimes go through very scary and difficult times in life (e.g., loss of a loved one, loss of a job, a traumatic assault or injury), when we suffer from situational depression, and need that little bit of help just to get through it. So no-one can responsibly declare anti-depressant drugs all good or all bad. Your doctor, or private counselor will have to guide you on this decision.

But, all can agree with the following, I am sure: **drugs alone are never a comprehensive enough treatment for depression or negative thinking**. For real, lasting change, there must be other changes, changes in our ways of thinking and behaving, if we are to get out of the old ruts. And, if you are dependant right now on high levels of anti-depressant, my hope would be that you can gradually get yourself down to lower levels, eventually even weaning yourself of the drugs, by tackling these other areas. In all cases, I ask that you please **only make changes in drug dosages after consulting with, and in agreement with, your physician or counselor.**

Some of those drugs are tricky, and need to be tapered off in a careful way, lest they cause a backlash effect in the system, or cause shock, due to sudden removal or reduction of something the system has learned to depend on.

Be forewarned: we hear a lot about the risk of suicide to people on the drugs. You might recall some negative publicity that Prozac, in particular, received in this regard – but Prozac is not the only drug that bears responsibility for this. Ironically, it turns out that those who reduce their levels after having been on high levels of anti-depressants are most at risk for this. Why? Because, as people emerge from drug usage, and become less 'doped up', they are capable of more initiative, and more assertive behavior. That's usually a good thing. However, should they have a sudden downward swing in mood, they are more capable of taking dramatic, disastrous action.

As has been said: **suicide is an extremely permanent solution to very temporary problems.** If by any chance you are entertaining suicidal ideas, please do the following, immediately: admit yourself to a hospital that is equipped to help you through this bad period and protect your safety. It's a voluntary admittance, thus you control how long you will stay there. But until you get through this very scary **TEMPORARY** period in your life, get the extra bit of help you need. Then, afterwards, a program like this can help you.

So, with regard to drugs: to do or not to do, that is the question.

You can come at this thing in a few different ways.

1.   You can take drugs. Period. Relying only on the magic pill, you pray that, with time, the depression lifts. Maybe, eventually, you'll be able to give up the drug. Sometimes this does, indeed, happen. Sometimes, depression will just lift, spontaneously. Sometimes not. But, this is looking a little too much like a roll of the dice. Preferable would be to take your own life in hand, and be assertive about how you'd like to live. Also: negative thinking will not spontaneously lift. For that, there's only one course – retraining of our minds. And to that purpose, you invested in this book.

2.   You can take drugs, trying to reset the chemical levels, to change your mood. You can decide to do this temporarily, while implementing this system (or, simply continue with a prescription already started), but plan on eliminating the drugs as the other factors are set into place.

3.   Assuming that the depression monster isn't very enormous right now, and you're not right between his jaws, you can use this system to reset your mood, which *should* reset the chemistry. There are some important conditions to the success of this, one of which is <u>consistency</u>, over time. Precisely because we are creatures of habit, we need to hold those new patterns steady for a while. Now, in the event that your current depression will obstruct implementation of our system properly, you may conclude that you need temporary help from drugs. That's no crime – rather you do that, to assist your success in this program, than to give up completely, and resign yourself to living forever with depression. But please do

plan to eventually rid yourself of the drugs, even as you plan to rid yourself of depression and negativity.

Situational versus Chronic, or Organic Depression

Something that may help you in the decision-making process about drugs, is to determine to what extent your depressions/negativity/bad moods are situational-dependent, and to what extent they are chronic. "How would I know?" you ask. Well, put this to the simple common sense test. Is your general affective state okay, for the most part, until you encounter a major experience that hits hard, throwing you into a slump (examples would be: stress at work, or employment struggles in general; financial stresses/scares/disappointments; loss, grief, etc; friction and tension in domestic relations, separation, divorce, etc)? Or, does the cycling of your moods seem unrelated to events? Almost regardless of whether things are going well or poorly, up or down, you find yourself unable to be positive-minded? This would be more descriptive of a chronic, or organic type of depressive state, and more amenable to drug treatment. Not that changes in mental pathways and behavioral patterns are unnecessary!!! In all kinds of depressive states, the interaction with events, relationships, your behaviors, and more will set up pathways that need re-programming.

So, in all likelihood, a combination of the two is called for: for the prescription, you will work with your doctor, or psychiatrist, for the other, I hope this program can be your solution!

I hope you can adopt the approach portrayed in these examples, of taking charge of your own health care, and directing it to where you would like it to be, rather than being reactive and allowing **it** to direct **you**.

The point of all this: there's an interactive process going on in our minds and bodies. A two-way street. We need to think more systemically, and orient ourselves towards a total change…a change of behavior, of thought patterns and mood, as will ultimately reset the chemical process, as well.

Now, a word about life. Of course, I realize that as you read this, and I speak to you, I know nothing about your personal circumstances. Those of you who suffered an awful tragedy in life, or have been dealt very hard blows in the past: If there's anyone who has legitimate cause to be depressed, it's you. You most certainly are deserving of sympathy, and admiration from the rest of us. As stated elsewhere in this book, "sometimes life is bigger than therapy". If there's anyone in society that has legitimate rights to be card-carrying, life members of the bitterness, or depression club, it's those who suffered terrible tragedies, illnesses, or painful childhoods. The real question here, however, is this: do you want to become a professional, eternal 'wounded' party? Why would you want to? It will not make the rest of your life easier – quite the contrary! This is the club to which you'd rather not belong. Groucho Marx once said: "I'd never join a club that would have me as a member." Think of it that way: the club of your entitlement to depression is not one to which you should want to belong.

So, much as I don't have a right to, I urge you, if these are your personal circumstances, throw away that club membership, and decide your future differently. You may not have control of the actions life performs on you, but you are in charge of your reactions from now forward.

YOU CAN REWRITE BEHAVIORAL CONDITIONING, SO THAT IT WORKS FOR YOU, NOT AGAINST YOU.

DEPRESSION IS NOT YOUR FRIEND. HE IS YOUR ENEMY, AND YOU CAN GIVE HIM THE BOOT!

And, as is true about all human areas of endeavor, the best way to increase our 'feel good' chemistry is the natural way – by thinking, behaving, and acting in 'feel good' ways. That's the purpose of this book: to shake up the system, to change the old patterns that included constantly slipping into negative or depressed states, and to ultimately help you eliminate that negativity, without dependency on drugs.

Chapter 5

Seeing the Monster in action

Seeing the theory in action in a 'real-life story'; understanding internal and external cues.

Let's see if we can apply some of the understanding gained in the earlier chapters to a 'real story' of someone suffering from depression. For the sake of this story, her name is 'Cindy'.

Cindy is a little baby, growing up in a normal American home. She has a mother and a father, and they live in an average home on an average block in an average city in one of the states of our country. However, there's a slight problem. Steven, Cindy's Dad, is unemployed since suffering an accident at the plant where he worked for ten years, supervising the manufacture of widgets. He needs to undergo surgeries, and to retrain, to enter a new profession that doesn't require him walking around a plant all day. Meanwhile, he's around the house, in a foul mood, suffering from physical pain and the psychological distress of feeling like a failed man. Because he's feeling low, he snaps at

Susan, Cindy's Mom, who snaps back. So now, poor little Cindy has both parents, always around the house, fighting much of the time.

Now, bear this in mind: we humans are made to be imitative creatures. We tend to copy others around us. It's how we learn, how we grow, and how we get on with our parents and friends. You've heard, perhaps, of patterning? It's that instinct, pre-programmed into baby ducks, to follow the first, big thing they see when they come out of the egg. 99.9% of the time, it works like a charm, because they follow, and automatically want to imitate, their mothers – she being the first creature they see. But, if you're unlucky enough to interrupt this process as chicks hatch, you'll have a trail of confused ducklings following you around, convinced that they are mini-versions of you! Trust me, it's true: the researcher who discovered this, a psychologist by the name of Konrad Lorenz, managed to convince many a poor little duck that it was born to be an experimental psychologist that looked like him and should follow him around for the rest of their lives!

Today, thanks to DNA and neural mapping, we even have a name for the neurons of the brain that program us to copy others around us: they're referred to as 'mirror neurons'.

It's a powerful, programmed human reaction. Without this ability, we would not acquire skills in life, learn how to communicate competently, or to sympathize with others. Thus, it's to be expected that Cindy will mirror the depressive state around her. With time, she will also internalize it, and it becomes the predominant mode of her internal world. As it repeats itself, thousands of times a day, the neural patterning is set up to keep it happening indefinitely. Also, with time, her chemical system will adjust itself to the mood around her and inside her, bringing about levels of neurotransmitters, adrenaline, and cognitive stimulation, that best suits this emotional and mental state.

Much of the time, Cindy is content to play with her dolls in her room, or to watch a children's show on TV. There are occasions, however, when she interacts with her parents — at the dinner table, or when they're in the living room together. Because Cindy is a responsive little human being, she picks up the depressed mood within the home, and she imitates the communicative style she is observing, which is snappy and negative. So, here's how that goes:
Mom says: "Cindy, come'n eat now."
Cindy responds in the manner she hears others using around her:
"I don' wanna eat now!"

Mom's inner response is shock, and indignation. It's enough that I have to put up with that from my husband all day! Darned if I'll take it from this little tyke. She angrily rebukes Cindy:

"Don't you give me lip, young lady. You get yourself over here and eat when I tell you to."

Cindy has run out of choices. She slowly and reluctantly walks to the kitchen, hikes herself up into her chair, and waits for supper. She can, however, pout and sulk through supper, and pick disinterestedly at her food, which is her way of 'getting back' at her mother. It's also the kind of response she sees her mother using when her father makes unpleasant remarks, or simply slumps around in a depressed state.

Cindy is about the most powerless person in the universe. She cannot express her anger, or resentment of the things that others are doing that hurt her. She's even told that she has no right to FEEL that way! She has only one other option: to turn it on herself, and feel sorry for herself.

So, imagine Cindy reacting in this manner to home situations, several times a day, every day of the week, over a few years. You've probably heard our neurological system described as "plastic". What does this mean? Well, simply put, plasticity indicates the flexibility of a system, its tendency to respond to, and be written by, behavioral patterns. In other words, it's sometimes difficult to tell whether behavior is being directed by neurology, biology and chemistry, or vice versa - whether it is dictating to them. Now, for most people, this is an inversion of their usual conceptions. We tend to think of the neural wiring, and the chemistry, as the 'hardware', sort of like basic equipment that cannot be changed, and behavior as the software that is determined by our basic hardware. Well, research, and modern science have changed our thinking about this, dramatically. We know, now, that it's a two-way street, that each of these components (physical features, like neurology or chemistry, and our responses, like actions or moods) can influence the other.

In Cindy's scenario, the depressive mood of the house and her mind, the example of her parents…all of it sets certain neural patterns in repetitive motion in her mental functioning, which also influence certain chemical 'neurotransmitter' levels, which strengthens, or reinforces her mood, which sets the repetitive neural patterns in place again…and around and around it goes, like an amusement park merry-go-round.

Something else happens inside Cindy. Since she gets no sympathy or support for how hard all this is on her, she sympathizes with herself. She tells herself – at a sub-conscious level - that she has a right to feel sad. She deserves to nurse and nurture her state of depression. She begins to see depression as her friend, the one that recognizes and validates her sadness and sense of loneliness. It's certainly more trustworthy than the people around her.

Now forty-five years old, Cindy lives and works in the big city. She is married to Bob, also 45, and has two children, a boy, 14, and a girl, 11. Cindy works for an import-export company, as an office manager/secretary. Perhaps she could be earning more, and should have received promotions, in terms of a title and pay-scale, since she runs the office single-handedly, however, her interactions with Mr. Gross, her boss, are unpleasant. She tends to be on the dour side, hardly ever smiles, and he always comes away from interactions with her feeling sort of…well, depressed. He doesn't know why, but he doesn't really like her, even though he knows that she is a good person, honest and reliable, and very good for his company. What he cannot know or understand, is that he reminds Cindy of both her father and mother, especially when he gives her orders and instructions. This calls forth a reaction inside her, quite beyond her control, pushing her into depressive states. She calls forth, in him, a responsive chord of sadness or depression — whatever level he carries inside as a result of his own life story. But, our concern is Cindy. Her constant reversion back to the passive aggression and helplessness of her childhood is preventing progress in her life.

Furthermore, on the domestic front, things aren't as great as they could be. Bob loves her, and she him, their kids are great, so no-one can figure out why they're not happy. Why is there such a cloud of sadness in the house? Why does Cindy, such an accomplished Mom, professional worker, and good person, seem so dissatisfied with herself, her marriage, and her home? Why can't she ever just relax, and have a good time?

Actually, she's too busy feeling sorry for herself. Life's challenges, diffi-culties and hard knocks cause her to withdraw to that same emotional place she was in at the kitchen table in her parents' home, and she reaffirms the "poor me" narrative she's got going on inside, the nursing and nurturing of how wretched life is, and, particularly, how wretched her life is.

External Cues.

The people around little Cindy, the girl, the atmosphere in her home, even the very home itself – these were all external cues, powerful enough to cause Cindy to feel depressed. An external cue is anything that has become associated with depression, which may have the power to actually trigger it. Sometimes, it's the actual cause of the depression to begin with – for example, Cindy's father, who is himself in a depressed state, and likely to spread it to anyone near him. With time, however, the very house can become an external cue, since it has housed the depressive atmosphere for so long, or a specific room in the house, or even an object, such as a doll that Cindy plays with in her room while trying to distract herself from events going on in the house.

Anyone who has worked to overcome a behavioral pattern can attest to the power of these external cues. Smokers working on quitting, for example, often have to stop going to the places in which they customarily light up; they may need to stop wearing certain clothes associated with the habit, and which trigger the desire, they certainly might have to give up drinking coffee, a frequent partner-in-crime with smoking.

A truly determined quitter will give up hanging with his friends — the company he kept when he was smoking. Likewise those recovering from alcohol addiction, drug use, and other such behaviors — they come to recognize that the triggers which entice the behavior are often extremely powerful — almost irresistible. Stay in that place, allow the power of the associations to mount, and it becomes kind of like standing at the top of a snow-covered, sheer ski-drop, your skis tipped and angled down, and saying to yourself "Aw shucks, I'll just resist the urge to slip down".

So, here's a simple question: why not block the urge before it starts, by avoiding that place, object, or situation, that triggers the impulse? Why not change patterns, places of 'hanging' and people to 'hang with', at least until you can develop a stronger resistance, and alternate responses to depression, self-defeat, or sadness? This of course gives you a hint at some of the steps and solutions we'll be presenting later in this book, which is fine, since the rationale should be very readily apparent to you by that point.
The powerful, magical secret for you to get is this:

WITH OLD, ENTRENCHED BEHAVIORS OR EMOTIONS, YOU GAIN MUCH MORE POWER AND CONTROL BY NOT LETTING YOURSELF GET TO HEAVILY-CUED SITUATIONS IN THE FIRST PLACE.

OR, AS THE OLD ENGLISH EXPRESSION HAS IT: AN OUNCE OF PREVENTION IS WORTH A POUND OF CURE.

LET'S TRY FOR THE OUNCE OF PREVENTION.

Internal Cues

Here's a sequence of events that should make sense to you from Cindy's story (and strike a few notes of familiarity from your own life):

Someone directs a few nasty, or critical comments at her; she begins to feel put-down and humiliated, so she makes a feeble attempt to resist, or stick up for herself. The response is of course an even more aggressive assault from the other, after which she is reduced to feeling utterly diminished and powerless, and she sinks into a deep depression.

The very first negative comment calls up all sorts of old associations in Cindy's mind: comments by her mother or her father, her sense of needing to defend herself and claim her place in the world. The even stronger response tips everything way over the edge of course, because by this point she's well into associations of her childhood. Furthermore, she's feeling like a girl of four or five, rather than a young lady of forty-five.

The feeling that Cindy first has when someone makes negative comment to her is an **internal cue** – it's a loaded sensation, like a train engine that will inevitably drag a whole bunch of cars loaded up with feelings and perceptions behind it. But, as Cindy gets dragged further into this, and feels demolished by the encounter – as New Yorkers would say: "forgedaboudit". She's gone. The chances of her being able to redeem herself with a sense of dignity and self-worth are between slim and none, and I'd bet my money on the none side. The internal cue is a feeling, a sensation, which by itself can act as a trigger for other sensations and frames of mind. Even harder to fight than the external cue, for one simple reason: how do you avoid an enemy you cannot see?

Most cases, this is an enemy you haven't yet identified, because unless you've done some serious psycho-therapy on yourself, you don't know what inner emotions and sensations are the triggers of your most negative emotional states. For years, Cindy endured situations where she was made to feel like a powerless, stupid little girl.

That, in addition to the fact that the general situation around her was very depressing – adults whose message was that this world is a mean place, where tough blows are dished out, and the only response available is to sit around a mope and complain. She has to have zounds of inner cues - these miserable associations that are waiting to be cued and come into play, like the philharmonic orchestra waiting for the conductor's baton – or any other well-rehearsed repertoire.

Furthermore, what she cannot possibly see, at this point in her life, is that she welcomes the depression, like an old friend. She invites it in, the moment she detects it lurking at the door. She is saying to herself, deep, deep inside where even she is unaware that it's happening: "I've earned this depression! I've gotten some bum raps here, and I'm gonna enjoy this depression, milk it for all it's worth!"

Sounds pretty bleak to you, I'm sure. But, here's the amazing part: it doesn't have to stay that way! Cindy has the capacity for change. Our minds are so eminently retrainable, our behavioral repertoires so responsive to new associations, that Cindy DOES NOT HAVE TO LIVE LIKE THAT FOREVER!!!

YOU CAN REWRITE BEHAVIORAL CONDITIONING, SO THAT IT WORKS <u>FOR</u> YOU, NOT AGAINST YOU.

DEPRESSION IS NOT YOUR FRIEND. HE IS A MUGGER, COMING TO STEAL YOUR SENSE OF WELL-BEING AND SELF-WORTH. HE IS YOUR ENEMY, AND YOU CAN GIVE HIM THE BOOT!

Do not ever let yourself reason that you have a right to be sad, or depressed. That's not a right, it's self-inflicted damage, disguising itself as your friend.

Chapter 6

Blowing the Monster to Hell and Gone

Our program: six easy steps to control your internal world, eliminate depression and negativity, and move towards self-empowerment.

Okay, you ready now to take on the Monster? I'll bet your trigger finger is just itching to blast him away. So, let's get started.

I hope, by now, you have internalized this message that we keep hammering away with: **DEPRESSION IS NOT YOUR FRIEND**. At the times that you're tempted to indulge yourself a little, to slip into the old, comfortable pose of slinking into an emotional 'corner', licking your wounds and sympathizing with yourself, you are surrendering to the enemy. Seductive, strangely attractive, perhaps. Familiar and comfortable, like old slippers. But depression is nonetheless a mean, ugly, big-toothed, bad-breath, stinky Mugger and Monster. He's the lousiest comfortable bed-fellow you ever don't want to get into bed with. Remember, hostages come to like their kidnappers, too, and often believe they're poor, misjudged individuals, their best friend while they're in captivity. Don't fall for this.

Time to send him to extinction, where he belongs!

So, here are your weapons. Get ready to stock up, cock 'n load, and blast away.

YOU'RE GOING TO WIN THIS WAR.

Say this to yourself. Out loud. Several times.

"I AM GOING TO WIN THE WAR ON DEPRESSION AND NEGATIVITY. I'M GOING TO KICK THEIR BUTTS TO HELL AND GONE!"

6-point program: SPAMGO.

Allow me to introduce you to **SPAMGO**. He will be your acrostic, and your weapon provider, for the day. Hopefully for many days.

And, just as we use aggressive protection against unwanted internet spam, you need aggressive protection against the enemy Depression before he gets in the gate.

Here's how it works:

Sense him – develop the ability to recognize depression's onset, early

Place – change your physical place

Action – change your behavioral repertoire

Mind – change your mind

And then, lastly, **Guard** against the monster sneaking around the gates, at all times, and cause an **O**ptimism to rule your internal world.

Step 1: SPAM – Sense him.

Unless we have consciously chosen to start paying close attention to our internal world, most of us cannot recognize the signs of depression setting in, until it is well entrenched. But, when it comes to beating off the monster, once we've allowed him to take up full residence, it's much harder to get rid of him. The power of this program is maximal when it is exercised pre-emptively; interrupting a monster depression *before* it manages to take control. So, how do we learn to recognize it?

There are those small, weak signals that it's coming on. Like before a storm, when you see darker clouds on the horizon, and you say to yourself: "Looks like it wants to rain." They feel like premonitions, tiny hints of the sense of darkness and despair on its way. Accepting the premise that depression is a response, these signs should almost feel like seductions, invitations to enter the world of depression with an old partner, the monster. Think of our example of Cindy, above, and her reactions to people, or situations that remind her of her childhood.

So, it's time to start paying attention to the people, things, moods…all the triggers that start you on the downhill slide. Some may be really simple. Like days of the week: some people get into a real slump on Mondays, which lasts until end of Tuesdays. Others crash downwards as the weekend approaches. End of day, beginning of day – whatever it is for you, learn to recognize it.

Other triggers will be complicated – like when a sequence of exchanges with someone leaves you feeling dejected, and you can't quite put your finger on why, and when it happened. Well, it's worth identifying what part of that sequence is your trigger, because once you've named all your triggers, you will be well armed to beat this monster.

So, what's needed now is careful watching, listening to your inner voice and even, if it would be helpful, recording. Keep a diary, noting your moods in response to times and events of the day. In particular, pay attention to those moments where you feel it can go either way: you can slide into depression, or you can turn the other way, get distracted from it, and by-pass the trap. So, the **S** of

SPAM is about learning to sense the dark mood before it sets in. Develop this sense. Perfect it. It's your powerful secret weapon, and it will give you distinct advantage over the enemy. SENSE him.

Step 2: SPAM: Change place.

Once you can recognize the depression in its early stages, a simple, and extremely effective move is to get up, and leave the place. Simply putting yourself in a new environment, with different external cues, can go a long way towards cutting Mr. Monster off at the pass. Once you come to recognize specific places that provoke the cues, try to avoid them, at least for a while, as you grow anti-depression muscles.

I hear you saying: "Hey, dummy, I can't avoid my workplace! Or my home! This is no plan."

Well, let's study that. There are ways to change your place without changing it. For example, change where you usually sit. If those yucky staff/board meetings depress you, announce to everyone that you prefer to be sitting at a different angle in the room "to gain another perspective!" Bring along a different chair, or cushion, that sits you up much higher. Tell them it's for your back. Or your legs. Or your neck. Gee, tell them anything! Shake things up a little. Become less predictable. Remember this: it's for your, and their, ultimate good, because if you become a happier person, in better control of your emotions, everyone gains. But, please, experiment. Move around a bit, and see what freedom you may actually have where you think you don't have any. Isn't it amazing the ridiculous reasons we stay the same, and do not exercise autonomy over our lives, year after year?

At home, you have more options than you realized. Eat dinner on the floor of the living room, with your kids, instead of the kitchen table, if you feel that's a downer. Eat on your bed, or the porch/deck/lawn. Redecorate your rooms. If you don't have budget for a total renovation, simply change around the furniture a bit. Shake things up. The whole idea is to confuse your inner world of cues and triggering, and to put yourself in charge. Do stuff you never dreamed of before. Work this matter creatively, and develop fast and nimble feet, so you can make your move in time, as you Sense the dark moments hovering. Confuse the heck out of them!

Step 3: SPAM – **Action**: Change your behavioral repertoire.

Like changing Place, discussed above, this is another really simple strategy – so simple, you're going to groan and say: "that's a strategy?" But yes, it is, and an extremely powerful one, at that. You see, you're looking to take a detour from your usual path, when the downhill slide begins, so that it gets interrupted before it starts, even. Trading Places is one way to confuse a mugger – you go somewhere else, unpredictably, so that he cannot get to you. The next is Trading Behaviors.

Here are a few examples: instead of sliding down into a miserable fight with your spouse/friend, just change the course of events. Say:

"Let's not discuss this matter now, not in this way. Let's rather put it off, just for a little while, and go have some really good ice cream!"

If the person you love resists you, and insists on doing this thing 'right now', explain to them what your tactic is. Assure them that you're not looking to avoid important matters, on the contrary, you want to start doing them better. So: "indulge me a little. Just let me try this. First we take a walk, we talk about nothing but the birds and the weather, for ten minutes, then we'll try again."

You can do the same with a boss, an employee, co-worker. Just choose to explain as much or as little as is appropriate.

"I have a favor to ask of you. Please go with me on this, for a little while. I may ask for a 'time-out' – a little break at unexpected moments. Indulge me, and I promise I'll come back to discuss whatever needed discussing. I just need to do this for the next little while for [health reasons] [personal reasons] [to get a grip on sanity]."

Would it be so bad to tell them that you're working on a new 'mental serenity' thing? Meditation? Whatever it is – and you have to be the judge of what would work best – isn't it worth a little extra effort and creativity to become self-empowered, much more in control, and much happier? Which is worse: a few moments of discomfort as people get used to your new weirdness and unpredictable nature, or a lifetime of negativity?

One more idea here: even if, for argument's sake, you cannot achieve any of the above, in terms of giving yourself the flexibility to change a course of action (though if that's the case, and you're really so powerless, I imagine you would not want to keep things that way for very long), there's still another option.

We can change our action protocol without re-arranging the environment, or other people. Remember those little hand exercisers, that provide tension against which you can resist, to build strength in the hands? Or, those 'squeegee' balls (kind of like racquetball balls) that were advocated as good therapy for dispelling tension, which we're supposed to squeeze repeatedly? Well, guess what: they work!

Let me explain why they work. Once you start to perform another activity which requires motor coordination, or logical thinking together with specific physical actions (a Rubik's cube is another example, or those little challenging games in which you have to roll balls enclosed in a plastic box into little holes), it causes the brain to activate the centers needed for that activity. In the case of a motor skill, that's the right side of the brain, rather than the left, and the parietal lobes instead of other centers. This will detract from the other areas being able to function, because our brains are not good at giving full attention to two very separate, different activities. In fact, we're terrible at it! This in effect shuts down the left side, which is our interpretive side, the one that can assign all sorts of negative meanings to what's going on. So, get the brain busy with a tricky hand-eye coordination, and you'll have avoided that slippery slope.

Here's a list of possibilities:

- Hand drawing: take up sketching on a little pad as a new hobby, and work on perfecting your skill at drawing a cup, bowl, or fruit.

- Rubik's cube, or a similar puzzle challenge.

- Take up shadow art, and practice the hand positions when you need to, or learn some sign language and practice it, going through the vocabulary you have acquired to test yourself.

- The 'Squeegee', or hand exerciser solution, or resistant play-dough (physical therapists can help you acquire this).

- Tennis ball, racquetball, squeezed between thumb and fingers.

- Elastic bands on fingers, pulled apart in repeated exercise

- Balance a pen or pencil on back of hand, try rotate it over fingers without use of the other hand.

Instead of sinking into a series of external and internal cues towards some dark place, you're going to start squeezing the heck out of some little rubber ball, or practice shadow art with your fingers, or some other goal-oriented, eminently distracting activity. Get out and find it. Check out your local sports stores, or medical supply stores. Study possible hobbies, crafts stores, etc. Think creatively. Try a tennis ball – nice, cheap solution. Or play-dough – take up animal shaping. Or origami (paper art) – though this one is a little more tricky, since it's doubtful you'll be able to whip it out and start doing at a moment's notice. Anything, just don't allow yourself to be boxed in to same ol' same ol', as if you have no free choice.

Remember Salman Rushdie? The great Indian writer who produced "Satanic Verses"? He risked his life, by writing and publishing a book that caused millions of people all over the world to want him dead. Price tags were put on his head, to raise the incentive for people to kill him. And he knew all this going in - he must have, for he was well familiar with the community he had angered – he had studied, and lived with them all his life. So the obvious question is: why did he do it? Why risk his life just to produce another book?

Well, as he himself has said, books are about 'opening perceptions'. They are about freedom of the mind. If we are all to be intimidated into surrendering our freedom, what value will life have at that point?

We cannot surrender our freedom, and, if we have relinquished some of it, we should work to take it back.

Step 4: SPAM: Change Your Mind.

When that thought process wants to take us down familiar old tracks, it is almost like a kidnapper, stealing our mental process from us. Well, guess what? You're going to launch a hostage rescue mission. You will not allow the kidnapper to get away with your mind; instead you'll take it back by "changing" your mind. What is meant by this?

What you need is a strong, compelling mental activity that is hard for you to resist, once started. Something that requires your full attention. Preferably something that is really fun, or funny, that might even get you laughing.

There's a neurological explanation for why this works: our brain, as amazing as it is, has limited resources at any given time. If we activate one area of the brain, the others will become subdued, to allow maximal blood flow. Think of your computer, and Random Access Memory – if we load it up too much, the whole system becomes muddled. So, working on this premise, if you can find a very distracting behavior for the moments at which your mind wants to go in directions you'd rather not, get it busy with something else.

Towards this end, I have included in this book as an Appendix (Appendix B) some of my favorite ditties of all time. They're silly little rhymes, picked up over the years – always good for a laugh. If you could possibly memorize these little poems, or jokes, so that you have them ready to trot out when the occasion warrants, they're practically guaranteed to divert your mind from where it was headed, and lift your mood. If you like, photocopy

them, and carry them with you everywhere, or write them into your
PDA, or computer. Here's a nice little example:

> *"See the happy moron!*
> *He doesn't give a damn*
> *I wish I were a moron.*
> *My God, perhaps I am!"*
>
> (anonymous)

Who could possibly hear that and not laugh?
Or, how about this one:
"There was an old man from Calcutta
> *(pronounced "Calcootta")*
Who fancied himself as a scooter
He rolled on his head,
For a board, used his bed,
And his rear end he used as a hooter"

To my thinking, only the brain dead would be able to resist
laughing at these silly compositions. And there are many more out
there — since taste, and humor, are irrational and indefinable things,
you're best off simply finding the ones that get you going. Check
out authors like Ogden Nash, or Shel Silverstein, or your local
Humor section in the bookstore.
Find them.

Your 'side busters', or 'knee slappers' – whatever you want to call them. Heck, make them up, if that works better for you! But collect them, put them on an index card, or something small like that, and carry it with you at all times. Or, use the ones provided in this program. Then, when things are beginning to look a little too bleak for comfort: don't go there! Just recite these ditties to yourself.

...CHANGE YOUR MIND...

Now, by the way, here's a fine alternative that some have used very successfully to do this 'alternate mental patterning'. Perhaps there's a list of things you need to know for work, or lists of names and phone numbers, or price lists, or technical terms of objects that you deal with daily. For me, for example, as a psychologist, it would be helpful to rehearse some of the diagnostic criteria for mental conditions, as described in the DSM (Diagnostic Statistic Manual). If you're a teacher, maybe you'd like to know the elements table better. Allied health, or medical profession? Go over your Anatomy, or drug info. Hey, if you like to follow sports, work on some averages, or records! Everyone has some item like this that they could benefit from knowing very well. Use these occasions to rehearse your lists – you'll be 'killing two birds with one stone', and you'll feel good about both benefits.

68

The important principles with the mental activity you choose are these:

> 1. It should be readily available, and take you no more than 1 second to whip out, or start reciting from memory.
> 2. It should be easy to start, in particular, but can rise in level of difficulty, so that there are no delays in getting started. Afterwards, if it gets challenging, that's not at all bad.
> 3. It should not be something that will frustrate, annoy or depress you. That would not make much sense, would it? To exchange one depressing thought process for another.

You, and only you, are Master of your internal world. Your mind. No-one else has the ability to control the paths down which your mind travels, and the state it is in. And if, perchance, you lost some of that control: hey,

TIME TO TAKE IT BACK.

Step 5: **Guard** The Gates.

Remember that you're up against a wily opponent. He's cunning, and creative. He will think of new ways to get in to your newly controlled mind. In fact, the more control you gain, the more desperate he will get in his efforts to take you back as his hostage again. Hell hath no fury as a lover scorned, and here, this dark enemy of yours was your friend and lover for many years, and you simply kicked him out of the sack!?? How dare you?

So, he's going to be lurking at every possible turn and twist, seeking to penetrate a wall, or find a loose bar in the gates, where he can sneak in. He's dying to see you crash and burn. He can't wait until you are lying and moaning before him, saying: "How on earth did I think I could escape you, Master? You're much too strong for me." Maybe you're having trouble envisioning this. Okay, let's go back to poor Cindy, and take another chapter from her personal book.

The new, renewed Cindy was a sight to behold! With a newfound confidence, she ran the company in an atmosphere of cheerfulness. She went about her day humming and singing, whenever she wasn't on the phone or busy concentrating. She had developed this strange new habit of laughing at her own jokes, obviously told to herself in secret. Kind of weird, you might say, but no-one cared, really. She was fun to be around. Her boss had given her a raise (she told him she'd leave otherwise), her husband was excited about new possibilities for their relationship, and her kids were much happier people. Until the day of that awful phone call.

Some jerk from Japan called up, angry about an order that had gone wrong. Perhaps because of cultural differences, or his grumpy mood, he misinterpreted Cindy's cheerful mood as scorning, or making fun of him and his problem. He went nuts! Demanded to speak to the boss, proceeded to cut Cindy to shreds, obnoxiously declared that he would not be doing business with them anymore…the whole nine yards. Cindy's first reaction was absolute shock. She looked like the proverbial deer in the headlights. Then she seemed to fold, like a crumpled paper cup. She went home early, climbed into bed and pulled the covers over her head, where she stayed for two days. Her thoughts?

'What was I thinking? How did I let myself believe that I could change things, or get away from myself? I will never amount to anything, and I will never escape this darkness that lurks within.'

You see, one of the mistakes we get into is assuming that, because we've put great effort into overcoming a major problem of our life, the world will gather around and applaud us, and decide to reward us from that day forward, by making things smooth-sailing. And if the world won't cooperate, well, obviously this plan was a bad one to begin with! Abort. Let me have my well-deserved sulk, thank you. Go away, turn off the lights, and leave me alone!

Unfortunately, the world has not changed everything for anyone yet, and isn't likely to start with you. Ogres will still be ogres. Miserable customers will still be out there. Someone will still appear, to cut you off on the highway, or steal your parking spot. Injustice still lurks at every turn of life, and selfish people will always be around to take advantage, or inflict damage on others. This does not mean that your resolution to change and improve yourself is 'against the karma of your life'.

As a matter of fact, it's likely that, as you effect changes in your life, things will get tougher, because the world generally abhors change, and it resists that change greatly. People who do find the resolve and courage to change find out, afterwards, that the battle has only just begun, because their personal reformation is resisted by hundreds of counter forces.

What has to change is the extent to which you allow yourself to be affected and reduced by these forces, and the extent to which you can shunt them aside, cauterize them in you own mind, side-step them and move on. So, you have to stand guard at every gateway to your mind, and be resolute in your decision not to succumb, ever again, to the second round of victimization – where your mind gets taken hostage.

Also, let's cut for ourselves a piece of wisdom pie from that which has been baked by the immensely successful recovery programs. Without question, one of the most heroic changes in life is overcoming addiction to substances – alcohol, or narcotics. This takes iron will, and firm resolution, because in a person who is prone to addiction, the substances have incredibly powerful pull. And one of the successful strategies that the programs advocate for staying away is to constantly be mindful of the fact that, once an addict, always an addict. That's why they speak up at meetings with:

"Hi, I'm Larry (or Alice/Sarah/Bob), and I'm an addict." **Because as long as that awareness is fresh, you're on guard against your enemy, the substance.**

Let your guard down, the vulnerability rises, and he can slip in and kidnap you.

Likewise, those of us that are prone to depression and negative thinking, or lived in it for a significant period of time, cannot ever let the guard down. Watch for him, because he'll be watching for his opportunity to move in on you.

The good news is that with time, he will eventually realize that there's no work for him around you, and he'll go away.

Until then, keep the gates well protected. How? Well,

- avoid the situations or people that can take you back there (This is real important: quit magical thinking. Stop convincing yourself that the person who always puts you down and makes you feel rotten won't do it this time because…[fill in the blank]. Thus, decide not to go to a party, much as part of you wants to, that has all the ingredients of your "7 on the Richter Depression Scale".)

- Anticipate its possible arrival in connection with an event – seeing an ex-spouse, getting results of a test, holidays with so-and-so – and guard against letting it happen to you, AGAIN.

Step 6: Optimism.

The next stage in this program may just be about the most powerful tool you can have, to reach full mood control. So much so, that I decided to dedicate a full chapter to it, alone.

Chapter 7

Step 6: Becoming **O**ptimistic

Step 6 in our six-step program is, without question, the most important. It is the action by which you can totally transform yourself, acquiring a new sense of power and resilience for life's knocks and challenges.

It calls for <u>some</u> work on your part: easy and enjoyable work, which will pay you back thousandfold in the long term for your little effort.

First, the theory behind this: a famous psychologist by the name of Martin Seligman is responsible for coming up with "learned helplessness" as well as "learned optimism". This is how it happened:

As a young experimental psychologist in the labs of Richard Solomon, at University of Pennsylvania, Seligman and the rest of the team faced a challenging problem. The project called for the conditioning of dogs to a negative stimulus – so, the dogs were receiving shocks together with hearing a high pitched sound. The plan was to later use the sound alone, as an adversarial stimulus. The problem was: the dogs became absolutely untrainable, for anything! A light went on in Seligman's head, and he wondered if the dogs had been 'trained to be helpless'. Since they could not get away from the shocks, they had learned that nothing they did could help, thus they simply despaired, after which they could not learn anything.

Seligman and other researchers who took interest in his approach quickly realized that they might actually be onto a model for the creation of depression in animals. He embarked on some historic studies that proved that whenever the dogs were given shocks, or anything noxious that they could not avoid or control, they gave up, and sank into depression. However, dogs exposed to the same amount of shock, with an ability to control it, remained sharp and active, and ready to learn more, despite being subjected to shocks. Further testing confirmed that the results could be demonstrated in humans (of course, the humans were not shocked; they were subjected to a loud, unpleasant buzzer. Also, please note that nowadays it is unlikely that an ethics committee of the university would approve shocking animals as they did back then). Seligman also found that the 'learned' helplessness was reversible: by actually, physically dragging the dogs past a barrier (they were supposed to be learning to jump over the barrier to get away from the shock), such that the shock then stopped, he taught the dogs that they could control the outcome, and they 'unlearned' their helplessness.

For Seligman and his team, the implications were huge:

- depression results when people cannot control the outcome of circumstances in their lives.

- Those who can affect outcomes may be able to withstand a great deal of stress without submitting to depression.

- People who 'give up' because they think they cannot possibly control outcomes can be retrained, and regain their ability to learn and not give up.

In further experimentation, it turned out that there was a factor missing in the application to humans. Dogs seem to learn to be helpless at almost a standard, universal doggie rate. However, when subjected to trying circumstances, some humans will 'learn helplessness' very soon, while others do not! How can that be? What gives some humans the ability to resist despair, even after repeated trials that convince them that they are powerless?

The answer came to Seligman and his teams after a while: it's all about what goes on in the head! Humans alter their reactions to trials through differences in interpretation. While some interpret the difficulties in a negative, or pessimistic way, others interpret them in an optimistic way. For example, some humans will react to a situation in which they cannot figure out a solution by saying to themselves:

"I'm such a monumental dummy, I'll never figure this out", and this pessimism will almost always be followed by despair, and a sense of depression.

Others, however, will say to themselves:

"What a stupid problem this is! No wonder I can't figure it out! It's stupidly designed." Or, they might think to themselves:

"No-one, in my circumstances, would be able to solve this one. That's okay: I'll solve the next problem that I get."

By ascribing the blame to something specific, outside of themselves, rather than something personal and pervasive (I'm such a dummy", or "my life is so rotten, I'll always have trouble", or, the other infamous Depression Driver: "Why do these things always happen to **ME**?"), they do not fall into a general sense of helplessness and low self worth.

Seligman took out his new theory for a test drive, and guess what: it works, and unbelievably so! By teaching humans the skills involved in being optimistic, he could train them to not give up, and to never become depressed. People who were formerly pessimists, and depressed, could easily be trained to act like optimists, and rid themselves of depression.

Here are those crucial skills:

Optimists Think:	Pessimists Think:
Temporary ("for now", or "this one") "I didn't do well on this one, but I'll do better next time."	**Permanent** ("I'm a dummy", "this'll never go away") "I'll never succeed in business, I just don't have it in me"
Specific ("this situation", "this person") "We're squabbling right now because we're both tired and upset. Tomorrow it'll be better."	**Pervasive** ("Always happens to me", "I'll never figure this out") "Our marriage is just miserable, always has been".
External ("their stupidity", or "poor system") "These customers need something else, that's why they don't buy from me."	**Personal** ("I, me, my...") "I'm just cursed – whatever I try to sell, they won't buy from me".

Let's play this out in a real-life example. Bryan, a sophomore student at American Town University, receives a 'C' on one of his exams, with some very critical comments from his professor. He goes into a slump, thinking to himself:

"I'm so stupid (personal, pervasive, permanent), how could I have believed I'd do well in law school?"

But, he has a good friend by the name of Buddy, who is always optimistic about life, who challenges his thoughts:

"Bryan, how can you say you're stupid? You got through high school with a decent GPA, didn't you? You got accepted to a good school. You're doing well on all your other courses, right? So, why would you call yourself 'stupid'?"

"I guess you're right, " Bryan responds, "but this professor is so damn demanding, and critical!"

"Oh, so it's the professor who's the jackass, not you, that's what you're saying?"

"I guess," says Bryan, laughing.

"So, Bryan", Buddy continues, "let's try to figure out why you didn't do well on that test. Did you study?"

"Yes. Maybe not as much as I should, but I did study."

"Okay, do you have all the materials; the notes, textbook, etc.?"

"Well," Bryan hesitates, looking a little sheepish. "I did cut class a little too often."

"So you're actually missing quite a bit of the info. Plus, the professor probably took offense with your not showing up, so he's giving it back to you. That's why he wrote such negative comments."

"Yah, you're probably right on that one. Never occurred to me."

"Okay, Bryan, so you're not going to waste another second on this funk! Come out with me for a beer, and tomorrow you'll go find the professor, ask him if you can do a make-up, or submit an extra paper. Let's go have some fun."

***

If only each of us had a friend named Buddy! Well, here's another idea: in the absence of a Buddy, you become your own buddy, by following his prescription. Notice what he does for Bryan:

1. He helps Bryan to express, and recognize, the negative thoughts that he's harboring in his head ("I'm so stupid").
2. He questions their logic, and brings counter-proofs ("You've done okay in school...doing okay in other courses. etc.")
3. He seeks other explanations, better ways (more temporary, specific and external) to explain the low grade, other than Bryan's stupidity (the professor, having missed class).
4. He lets it go, distracting himself with a fun, positive activity.

Here's the prescription for a more **optimistic** you:

1. Recognize your internal speech, and the things you attribute problems to. Pay attention to the 3 P's: Permanent, Pervasive and Personal.
2. Argue with the permanent, pervasive, personal explanations, by bringing counter-proofs. Show yourself where you've handled similar things well, or how life has actually blessed you.
3. Seek different explanations for unpleasant outcomes that are: temporary, specific, and external.
4. Move on. Do something positive, and do not dwell on the negative.

Got it? Good. Now, you have to apply it. Let's try some role-playing with this.

Make a list of some of your more negative moments in life. It doesn't have to be a long list – five or six items will do (a few examples are provided below). Next, you will close your eyes and imagine yourself in the situation. Make it come alive, by feeling the experience, as strongly as possible. Listen to your inner voice: what are you saying? How are you explaining the circumstances to yourself? Apply the four principles outlined above to be optimistic, instead of pessimistic.

Here are some examples of the kind of situations you might want to work through:

- Your boss passes you, doesn't say a thing about you coming in early, or working so hard on your project, and instead insults you about how you're talking on the phone.

- Your child comes home from school, you ask him how he liked the lunch you made him, and he says: "Yucky. I didn't eat any of it."

- Someone shoves ahead of you in line in the grocery store. You ask the cashier to prevail, and to honor your being first, and she simply brushes you off. The other customer goes away with a smirk on her face.

- You're telling one of your parents about your efforts in your career, and he/she says: "Well, obviously you're not doing so well there – I told you you were not suited for that job."

o   And so on, as appropriate for your life.

- -

Flood yourself with positive feelings and associations:

Relative to the last point: easier said than done, right? How do we distract ourselves from negativity and upset, after a bad event?

We've been talking a great deal about the power of negative associations to form in our very pliable, malleable minds. And the stress in this program has been on taking the same force that made these associations so strong, to use against the negativity and **for** yourself. Here's a method for 'moving on', for flooding yourself with positive and encouraging thoughts, instead of negative ones:

- -

■   Pavlov showed us, in his famous experiments with dogs, that if the stimuli and the reinforcers are strong enough, associations can be made very quickly, and quite powerfully, such that they will last for a long time.

■   No matter how strong the associations formed in us between two events, or objects, over time they will fade, provided stronger ones replace them and are repeatedly reinforced.

- -

What this means is that:

- -

(1)   When you choose to be the architect of your own associations, they can form quickly and powerfully.

(2)   If you repeat them many times, they will become more dominant than the old ones.

So, how can we engineer our own associations? It's easier than you think. Here's what you need to do:

- Select a beautiful piece of music. This can be something you already know and love, provided it's not crowded by too many personal memories (since we don't want any nostalgia creeping in here). If you need to find something for yourself that has no prior associations, try the 'New Age' section of your music store, unless you're a classical music listener – those media are great, because they have no vocals, which reduces the extraneous connections.

- Select an activity and place that give you maximal pleasure. Perhaps that's in your bedroom, getting a back-rub from your spouse. A soak in the tub? Maybe simply relaxing in your favorite chair, when all is quiet and you can truly let all worries go. Maybe a good, old-fashioned glass of sherry, or chocolate liqueur, to 'mellow' you out, or any other treat that you really enjoy. You could also read a book at the same time, provided the contents will be a source of calm and enjoyment for you, not tension. If you are doing this alone, consider having some favorite photographs to look at, of a person/people who gave you great comfort and joy.

- If you do not already have one, look into procuring an ipod, mp3, or any other portable music player. Your objectives are: portability, and convenience – in the smallness of the device. Our kids have this one down pat: your music player has to be small enough to fit in your pocket or on your hip comfortably.

You want to listen to the music only in relaxing, pleasant circumstances at first, many times over. In this manner, you will build positive associations with the music. Then, you will use the music and its associations at the moments when you need to flood your mind with positive thoughts, creating an overflow that will ward off all negativity.

This part of the plan is very important. Do not dismiss the potential benefits of this, for it can be a very powerful tool. We tend to think that memories and associations formed against our will are overpowering, and those that we form or construct are 'wimpy' in comparison. This is not true. Repetition is a crucial key here, together with careful selection of the tools for setting those memories.

There. Now you have it. The entire program.

S.P.A.M. G.O.

S – <u>Sense</u> the presence of depression or negativity, before it infiltrates,

P – Change <u>Place</u> to the extent that you can, selecting a different environment, or position.

A Change your <u>Actions</u> – Establish new behavioral repertoire, and implement it quickly and effectively, when needed. Keep it going in the critical situation, to block negative patterns.

M – Change your <u>Mind</u> – avoid dark pathways in your mind, by detouring yourself to other, more joyous pathways, with mental exercises that distract you from the road leading to depression.

G – <u>Guard</u> against the return of the negativity, with vengeance, and remain forever vigilant against his return.

O – Become an <u>Optimist</u>, by changing the process you use to explain situations and problems in life.

The rest is up to you: study the elements of this program, memorize the code of **SPAM GO**, and you can definitely change your life for the better.

Appendix A, at the end of this book, provides the CES-D questionnaire again. Fill it out approximately two months after implementation of this program. By comparing your score this time with your first score, you will have some idea what changes have come about in you as a result of taking the program. You can also re-administer to yourself whenever you choose – just leave some gap of time (two months is the minimum advocated) between testings. Good luck!

Consistent, determined application of this program **can** change your life, and put you on the road towards much more positive mental process, as well as happier and more productive interactions with others. With time, furthermore, and constant growth in mastery of the strategies outlined here, you can banish depression from your life completely, and live in happiness, drug free, hopefully for a long, long time.

Chapter 8

A father figure in both depression and cognitive psychology, Aaron Beck believed that many depressive states can be traced to a faulty, negative thinking process. Call them 'missteps' in logic, or erroneous conclusions, they cause people to reach incorrect and upsetting conclusions that are harmful to their confidence.

Beck identified **five** such errors, the ones that show up most often. They are:

Arbitrary Inference:

Whenever we draw a conclusion that has very little evidence to support it, we make an arbitrary inference. Here's an example: a young schoolchild goes in to see the principal, speaks with him, and then prepares to leave. It seems as if the principal is rushing to get rid of her, from which she concludes that he doesn't like her. In fact, the cause for the impatience could be many more pressures on the principal that she's unaware of, or the fact that he does not want her to be late for class. She is making an inference, a leap of logic that is unsupported, based on which she may become unnecessarily depressed; furthermore, since she's unlikely to ever question her conclusion with the principal, her relationship may forever be tainted by this encounter. **The Solution?** To carefully examine our conclusions, and identify whether they are based on solid evidence from several sources, or drawn from a misreading of the situation.

Selective abstraction: Sometimes, we have a tendency to focus on one aspect, or piece of a large picture, to the exclusion of all else, and we reach incorrect conclusions as a result. For example, imagine a worker who is generally liked and appreciated by all, but has a frictional interaction with one co-worker. With time, he becomes preoccupied with that one frictional relationship, and assumes that 'nobody likes me in that place'. A typical example where this happens is where a person receives a very positive evaluation, or lavish praise on their performance, but within that approval comes one critical comment that calls for improvement. Instead of responding to the positive with appreciation, and promising to work on the other, this person can choose to 'stew' on the negative, and become very resentful, feeling unappreciated. This is another error in mental processing. The error is often rooted in having been harshly criticized as a child, and not having the ability to tolerate even gently-delivered criticism graciously.**The solution?.** To learn to isolate the negative, see it in perspective, and train oneself in gracefully tolerating negative comments from others. Role-playing this with a close friend can be very helpful.

Overgeneralization Similar to the two examples above, this error involves a person drawing a general conclusion based on one incident or experience. Scientists know that it's very misleading to reach a conclusion based on one incident, for exceptions to the rule must be allowed for in every rule. Even the 'almost perfect' person makes mistakes - what happens if we judge them based on that one mistake, instead of overall performance? So, let's say that a person starts a new job, and is learning many new skills, but makes a major mistake in one of their new tasks. Drawing the conclusion: "I'm useless, I'll never learn this stuff," is of course unwarranted. We need to be able to keep a larger perspective, and stand back a little bit, even where this invovles ourselves directly, to reach sound appraisals of ourselves and our relationships.

Magnification and Minimization For some, a small, negative event can be dismissed as unimportant and irrelevant to the overall story of our lives. Unfortunately, that's not true for all. Some will tend to dwell on and exaggerate the meaning of a negative event, and to minimize the big, good one. Here's an example: imagine a girl has just announced her engagement. Her entire family is thrilled, her fiancee and his family are thrilled. Celebration is in the air! Then she goes to work, where everyone is coming over and congratulating her, wishing her well. She notices that one co-worker refuses to even acknolwedge her joyous event, or wish her well. With time, this rankles her, and rattles around inside her. Yet, the cause may have nothing to do with her. Perhaps this other person was herself deeply disappointed by a failed engagement, or devastated by the divorce of her parents, causing an inability in her

to rejoice with someone else's joy. It has little to do with our blush-
ing bride, everything to do with the other individual. But, if she
allows, the 'bride' could dwell on this as if there is nothing else.
This is a case of the 'missing tile' syndrome - dwelling on the tile
that's missing, being unable to see the rest of the tilework, no matter how beautiful.

Personalization Each of us is the center of our own world, and
sometimes we become convinced that the world sort of revolves
around us. This can be a trap, when it comes to logical thinking,
because we are not really the cause or target of everything that
happens. Say, for example, bad weather causes a collision, resulting
in serious injury to two drivers, just as I'm about to cross the street.
I can convince myself that it was because I was there, or stepped
off the curb, that the accident happened, thus I am to blame for
the injuries. Yet, many factors might have contributed to the event:
carelessness of one of the drivers, slow reflexes or distractedness
of another, poor road conditions or a glare, unclear road signs, and
more. But, the personalizer discounts all these issues, seeing only
themselves in the situation.

In all of the above circumstances, Beck would want to counsel the
individual to study their assumptions and conclusions, so they can
begin to see the faulty steps in their logic that are leading to these
false conclusions and unwarranted depressive states.

You might ask: why were these "errors of logic not included in the above SPAMGO formula somehow?" Good question. Although it would certainly be helpful to become aware of these 'dead-end pathways' of the mind, and start to alter patterns of thinking when you find yourself leaping to unfounded conclusions, this is not necessarily the most powerful way to change moods and patterns. Reconditioning, as described in Chapter 6, and Optimism, as described in Chapter 7, will probably be the most effective approach for quick results. Over time, however, it would do to be aware of the conclusions you are reaching or jumping to, so try to remember Beck's five errors, as well, and evaluate the bases on which you reach or arrive at impressions and decisions.

Chapter 9

In this chapter, we cover a collection of practical issues: diet, physical fitness, personal interactions and the like, which can impact upon your state of mind.

Physical Fitness, Exercise, and Mental Framework

Earlier in the book, we spoke about the incredibly positive effects of physical exercise, and the benefits it can bring. Get this: in studies comparing people using the traditional anti-depressants (tricyclics, etc.) with others who only got physical exercise, it was found that equal benefit was obtained by those who exercised regularly as those who were on a prescription. Imagine that! Simply exercising three or four times a week was equal to the best pre-scriptions out there in banishing depression. Now, which do you think is better: to shove a drug into your body whose full effects and repercussions are not well understood or known, or to get some physical exercise, benefiting your heart, blood pressure, your figure, length of your life, as well as your mood? Dah, let me think about this one…

The problem facing those who are not on any sort of fit-ness program is of course this:

"I'm feeling too depressed to work out, but I need to work out to feel good enough to want to work out…?" A Catch 22 if ever there was one. For this, there are several simple pieces of ad-vice:

- Start real small. Bargain with yourself that you're going to get on the treadmill, or walk outside, for 5 minutes, no more, and walk very slowly, at 2.5 miles per hour. That's all you will try to do the first day. The second day, 6 minutes, at 2.6 miles per hour. Maybe skip a day, then do 7 minutes, at 2.7. And so on. What you might find is that once you're in the swing of it, you'll be reluctant to stop, so you'll go for another minute or two, and you may even raise the speed a notch. As long as you don't overwhelm yourself at the beginning, you'll find it easy, and enjoyable, to continue with what you're doing, and the improvement will come sooner than you think. Patterning, and repetition will start working with and for you…but you know all about that by now, you're an expert already.

- Consider getting a trainer, at least for the very beginning. It's much easier when we have an 'external cue', prodding and motivating us to get started, and to keep going. If you cannot afford a trainer, consider recruiting a friend or family member, to accompany you on your first few sessions at the gym or on the equipment. Get someone positive, who can encourage you with lots of compliments or rewards. If you don't have anyone like that in your 'inner circle', make them! Groom and prepare them, by being very specific about what you want from them

Diet.

Are there foods that are worse for depression/negative mindsets, and some that are better? You bet!

As you might expect, foods that are generally good for you are better for positive frames of mind, and those that are bad for you will promote negative frames of mind. Here are a few examples:

- Fatty foods are hard on the body for digestion, and will often slow the mind down, bringing about a sluggish feeling throughout the body, which the mind could interpret as a depressed state.

- Caffeine or sugar, while causing an initial 'high' (with sugar this happens within minutes, with caffeine it is strongest in the first hour after consumption), will cause a 'melt down' later, bringing about fatigue and a depressed frame of mind. The cycle for sugar is about an hour or two to melt-down, and with caffeine, it is between three and four hours, depending on amount consumed. Alcohol, by the way, does the opposite: initially we feel mellowed, a pleasant, light buzz. But later (2-4 hours), we tend to wake up and become agitated, heart beating faster, etc.

- Likewise, when it comes to carbs, we're always better off with low Glycemic Index foods, and slow release carbohydrates (or, in the newest terminology that tracks the carbs in foods, low Glycemic Load - GL), for similar reasons to those specified for sugar, above. High GL foods cause sudden, intense release of sugar into the system, followed by what feels like a sudden depletion, while low GL foods provide us with more gradual, prolonged sustenance, with less likelihood of the after-ball drop.

Omega -3 Magic.

Turns out that the Omega -3 acids are good for a gazillion things, including mood and mental set. One of the best natural sources of this is of course, fish, but not all fish are created equal. There are good fish and bad. According to the Network of Environmental Defense, these are the 'good' fish, which provide excellent amounts of Omega 3 without contamination or harmful by-products:

Abalone (if farmed in the U.S.); Anchovies (watch your sodium intake here); Arctic char, when farmed; Catfish, when farmed; Halibut (Alaskan); Herring (Atlantic); Mackerel (Atlantic); Mahimahi (Atlantic), fresh salmon (from Alaska or U.S. farmed) as well as canned; sturgeon (U.S. farmed); Tilapia and Tuna – especially the fresh form, but limit your intake, since tuna has high levels of mercury.

Some 'bad' fish: Chilean seabass, Grouper, Atlantic salmon, Rockfish/cod from the Atlantic or Pacific; Wild Caviar; imported shrimp or prawn; imported swordfish or bluefin tuna, and shark. (See www.environmentaldefense.org)

Then, of course, there's the simple solution of taking Omega 3 supplement, in the form of pills or liquid; just do your research to be sure that you're relying on reputable companies for your supplements.

The B-Complex, Vitamins C and E, and SAM-e.

The other supplements that have been documented to benefit mood are the B-complex, always advocated as good defense against stress, in any event. Vitamin C, likewise, boosts our immunology and defense against viral and other physical stressors, while improving our sense of wellbeing. Vitamin E, as well, is supposed to help regulate positive moods, in addition to all its other benefits (anti-oxidant, skin support, etc.).

Then there's SAM-e (S-adenosylmethionine), about which there are many claims of its benefit to mood. The premise behind it is that some people's bodies may not produce enough of the substance, which is crucial for the body's processing of methionine, an amino acid (yet another neurotransmitter!). We leave it to the reader to ascertain for yourself whether these claims are valid or not, and what level of scientific substantiation of the claims has been performed.

Also new to the world of therapy for depression and 'negativity' is 5-HTP. The claim is that this substance acts as a precursor to serotonin, so that taking it will increase the production of serotonin. Of course, the claim that this is a 'more natural' manner of boosting your serotonin should not be taken seriously: any manner in which we manipulate the natural production of substances in our body with a chemical or substrate, call that product natural or not, is artificial. Besides, aren't we all familiar with people becoming sick due to over-exposure to some product, natural or not? E-coli is natural, if you must know, so is salmonella, bacterial or fungal culture, and fermentation. Thus, the claim "natural" should not automatically induce a sense of safety.

As many are by now aware, St. John's Wirt enjoyed a long run, with all sorts of claims about its "natural" therapeutic effects, many of which have been refuted. At this point, many are convinced that it is useless, but others claim that it truly does help lift their darker moods. I guess, on this subject, it's "every man for himself".

Meditation: A powerful mood resetter.

As one who has practiced and taught meditation for many years, I can testify that this is an amazing vehicle for transformation of the internal world. The regular practice of meditation can endow us with serenity, a sense of calm, improved attention, much more masterful control of our thought and mood process, improved blood pressure, calmer heart rates, and much more. An extremely impressive list of physical and mental functions have been scientifically documented to improve with meditation. How does it work? Well, just as sleep is a magical process that somehow rejuvenates and resets the body in ways not fully understood or identified, so can meditation. The practiced meditator becomes adept at altering the frequencies of his/her brain waves, putting the self into a state within which repair and rejuvenation are generated for all of our body's cell matter, and there is a 'resetting' of the electrical impulses generated in our nervous system. Also, by accessing the sub-conscious, the meditator opens up creative process of thinking and feeling, that they might not have been able to access otherwise.

To find out more about avenues to develop this amazing skill, including retreats and home-study courses, log on to an additional website at:

www.free-psychotherapy-advice-online.com
Click on "Meditation"

*   *   *   *

Thank you for having made this purchase. We are pleased that you took this assertive action to change your life, and gain control of your inner self. We feel privileged to have been partners with you in this journey, and wish you much luck and continued success in all your endeavors.

For those who feel it would be easier to implement the 6-step program of this book in the setting of a live seminar, in order to boost yourself faster towards success, please check this out at:

www.free-psychotherapy-advice-online.com

Appendix A: Follow-up Quiz.

Administer this quiz to yourself again, about two months after implementing the 6-step program in your life.

Answer these questions as relative to the past week. During the past week:

1. I was bothered by things that usually don't bother me.

0 – rarely or none of the time

1 – Some or a little of the time (1-2 days)

2 – Occasionally or a moderate amount of the time (3-4 days)

3 – Most or all of the time (5-7 days)

2. I did not feel like eating; my appetite was poor.

0 – rarely or none of the time

1 – Some or a little of the time (1-2 days)

2 – Occasionally or a moderate amount of the time (3-4 days)

3 – Most or all of the time (5-7 days)

3. I felt that I could not shake off the blues even with help from my family and friends.

0 – rarely or none of the time

1 – Some or a little of the time (1-2 days)

2 – Occasionally or a moderate amount of the time (3-4 days)

3 – Most or all of the time (5-7 days)

4. I felt that I was not as good as other people.

0 – rarely or none of the time

1 – Some or a little of the time (1-2 days)

2 – Occasionally or a moderate amount of the time (3-4 days)

3 – Most or all of the time (5-7 days)

5. I had trouble keeping my mind on what I was doing.

0 – rarely or none of the time

1 – Some or a little of the time (1-2 days)

2 – Occasionally or a moderate amount of the time (3-4 days)

3 – Most or all of the time (5-7 days)

6. I felt depressed.

0 – rarely or none of the time

1 – Some or a little of the time (1-2 days)

2 – Occasionally or a moderate amount of the time (3-4 days)

3 – Most or all of the time (5-7 days)

7. I felt that everything I did was an effort.

0 – rarely or none of the time

1 – Some or a little of the time (1-2 days)

2 – Occasionally or a moderate amount of the time (3-4 days)

3 – Most or all of the time (5-7 days)

8. I felt hopeless about the future.

0 – rarely or none of the time

1 – Some or a little of the time (1-2 days)

2 – Occasionally or a moderate amount of the time (3-4 days)

3 – Most or all of the time (5-7 days)

9. I thought my life had been a failure.

0 – rarely or none of the time

1 – Some or a little of the time (1-2 days)

2 – Occasionally or a moderate amount of the time (3-4 days)

3 – Most or all of the time (5-7 days)

10. I felt fearful.

0 – rarely or none of the time

1 – Some or a little of the time (1-2 days)

2 – Occasionally or a moderate amount of the time (3-4 days)

3 – Most or all of the time (5-7 days)

11. My sleep was restless.

0 – rarely or none of the time

1 – Some or a little of the time (1-2 days)

2 – Occasionally or a moderate amount of the time (3-4 days)

3 – Most or all of the time (5-7 days)

12. I was unhappy.

0 – rarely or none of the time

1 – Some or a little of the time (1-2 days)

2 – Occasionally or a moderate amount of the time (3-4 days)

3 – Most or all of the time (5-7 days)

13. I talked less than usual.

0 – rarely or none of the time

1 – Some or a little of the time (1-2 days)

2 – Occasionally or a moderate amount of the time (3-4 days)

3 – Most or all of the time (5-7 days)

14. I felt lonely.

0 – rarely or none of the time

1 – Some or a little of the time (1-2 days)

2 – Occasionally or a moderate amount of the time (3-4 days)

3 – Most or all of the time (5-7 days)

15. People were unfriendly.

0 – rarely or none of the time

1 – Some or a little of the time (1-2 days)

2 – Occasionally or a moderate amount of the time (3-4 days)

3 – Most or all of the time (5-7 days)

16. I did not enjoy life.

0 – rarely or none of the time

1 – Some or a little of the time (1-2 days)

2 – Occasionally or a moderate amount of the time (3-4 days)

3 – Most or all of the time (5-7 days)

17. I had crying spells

0 – rarely or none of the time

1 – Some or a little of the time (1-2 days)

2 – Occasionally or a moderate amount of the time (3-4 days)

3 – Most or all of the time (5-7 days)

18. I felt sad.

0 – rarely or none of the time

1 – Some or a little of the time (1-2 days)

2 – Occasionally or a moderate amount of the time (3-4 days)

3 – Most or all of the time (5-7 days)

19. I felt that people disliked me.

0 – rarely or none of the time

1 – Some or a little of the time (1-2 days)

2 – Occasionally or a moderate amount of the time (3-4 days)

3 – Most or all of the time (5-7 days)

20. I could not "get going".

0 – rarely or none of the time

1 – Some or a little of the time (1-2 days)

2 – Occasionally or a moderate amount of the time (3-4 days)

3 – Most or all of the time (5-7 days)

Appendix B: Limerick Fun

See the happy moron!

He doesn't give a damn

I wish I were a moron.

My God, perhaps I am!

(anonymous)

There was an old man from Calcutta

Who fancied himself as a scooter

He rolled on his head,

For a board, used his bed,

And his rear end he used as a hooter

(by: none of your business)

There once was a man from Quebec

Who tied both his legs round his neck

Like a fool he forgot

How to untie the knot

And now he's an absolute wreck

(anon)

There once was a man in Peru

Who dreamt he was eating his shoe

He awoke with a fright

At the stroke of midnight

To find out that it was true

(anon)

There was a farmer from Leeds,

Who ate six packets of seeds,

It soon came to pass,

He was covered with grass,

And he couldn't sit down for the weeds!

> (anon)

An epicure dining at Crewe

Found a very large bug in his stew.

Said the waiter, "Don't shout

And wave it about,

Or the rest will be wanting one too."

> (anon)

There was a young woman named Bright

Whose speed was much faster than light.

She set out one day

In a relative way,

And returned on the previous night.

> (anon)

There once was an old man of Esser,

Whose knowledge grew lesser and lesser,

It at last grew so small

He knew nothing at all,

And now he's a college professor.

> (definitely anon)

There was an old lady from Clyde

Who ate forty apples and died

The apples fermented

inside the lamented

and made cider inside her insides

(anon)

There was a young maid from Madras

Who had a magnificent ass;

Not rounded and pink,

As you probably think---

It was grey, had long ears, and ate grass.

(anon)

There once was a lady named Lynn

Who was so uncommonly thin,

that when she assayed

to drink lemonade,

she slipped through the straw and fell in!

(by G.M. Woodhouse)

There was a young man named Wyatt

whose voice was exceedingly quiet

And then one day

it faded away

...

(by Spike Milligan, English comedian)

Troubleshooting:

In the event that you are having difficulty implementing the program, or seeing adequate results, please try the following:

As a mechanic would, you'll go over the entire system to see where the glitch is. Carefully evaluate each component:

S. – are you vigilant enough in sensing early onset of a depressive mood?

P & A. – when you sense it coming on, are you prompt in changing what you are doing and where?

M. – have you taken adequate steps to allow you to make a quick 'change of mind'? Did you rehearse with pleasing music, or memorize something that you can practice at that critical moment?

G. – are you vigilantly guarding all gates against the re-entry of that wily, evil mood?

O. – have you worked on the rules of optimism, making your self reflections regarding unfortunate events **specific, temporary**, and **external**, rather than **personal, pervasive, permanent**?

Revise your system, methodically, until you identify the weak spots, and then work assertively at strengthening and reinforcing the points where it is needed.

If at first you don't succeed, please do not give up, but try and try again. After all, you'd do that much for your car, if its idle was acting funny, wouldn't you? You'd go back to the dentist, if that crown wasn't sitting right. Give it a chance, because it will work for you, if you work on it. Best of luck!

<u>Notes:</u>

Notes:

<u>**Notes:**</u>

Response Form:

I'd really like to hear from you!

Please fill in the form that appears below, then cut carefully around box to detach (tearing out the page will weaken the binding of the book), and either fax or mail back to us at GTN Publications.

Name:	
Address: (optional: add email address if you wish)	
Comments regarding book:	
Fax to us at:	410-358-4790
Or mail to:	GTN Publications, P.O.Box 65203, Baltimore, MD 21209 Write to us on the Web: www.free-psychotherapy-advice-online.com

gtn

www.ingramcontent.com/pod-product-compliance
Lightning Source LLC
Chambersburg PA
CBHW030025290326
41934CB00005B/492

This is the ultimate manual in eliminating depression and negative thinking. Through simple terms, complex concepts are explained, putting readers in charge of their internal moods. Included: a self-administered depression test, the author's 6-step SPAMGO system for empowerment, dietary and other influences on mood. The book draws from current psychological research, including: Cognitive Behaviorism, Mindfulness, Learned Optimism, Neuropsychology.

Dr. Gabriel Newman is a Rabbi and practicing Psychotherapist residing in Baltimore, Maryland. He holds a Ph.D. in Psychology, and is a licensed Clinical Family and Marital Therapist with the Department of Health and Mental Hygiene of Maryland. He draws from his many years of clinical experience with grief and personal loss, and current research.

"Dr. Newman has created a simple step-by-step approach, based on solid data, to rid oneself of depression, which is so common and at times overwhelming. This is a unique, self-directed approach which will have great utility to my patients." Dr. Stephen Glasser, Baltimore, MD

"How to Eliminate Depression and Negative Thinking by Gabriel Newman PhD is a welcome small volume with a much needed big message. It is accessible, draws on legitimate behavioral science, and uses an easy to follow step by step method. This book has already proven useful to me as an internist trying to assist patients replace pessimism with positive thinking. I know how important optimism is to their recovery. I recommend a careful reading and re-reading of Dr. Newman's book to patients and families wherever depression is an issue." Harry M. Walen M.D., Baltimore.

ISBN 978-0-6151-4354-5

ID: 755178
www.lulu.com

9 780615 143545